# 24 Piano Transcriptions of Classical Masterpieces

## From Orchestral, Operatic, Vocal, & Chamber Works Transcribed for Advanced Piano by Robert Schultz

Second Edition

*Alfred's Classic Editions*

D1082223

*Editor: Robert Schultz*
*Contributing Music Editor: Dr. Tina Faigen*

Copyright © MMVIII by Alfred Publishing Co., Inc.
All Rights Reserved. Printed in USA.
ISBN-10: 0-7390-5356-6
ISBN-13: 978-0-7390-5356-0

# Table of Contents

ADAGIO IN G MINOR
Tomaso Albinoni (1671–1750) . . . . 4
AIR (from *Orchestral Suite No. 3*)
Johann Sebastian Bach (1685–1750) . . . . 10
AVE MARIA
Giulio Caccini (1545–1618) . . . . 15
AVE MARIA
Franz Schubert (1797–1828) . . . . 48
CANON IN D
Johann Pachelbel (1653–1706) . . . . 22
CASTA DIVA (from *Norma*)
Vincenzo Bellini (1801–1835) . . . . 43
DANCE OF THE BLESSED SPIRITS (from *Orfeo ed Euridice*)
Christoph Willibald Glück (1714–1787) . . . . 32
EIGHTEENTH VARIATION (from *Rhapsody on a Theme of Paganini*)
Sergei Rachmaninoff (1873–1943) . . . . 109
INTERMEZZO (from *Cavalleria Rusticana*)
Pietro Mascagni (1863–1945) . . . . 79
KOL NIDREI
Max Bruch (1838–1920) . . . . 68
LA MAMMA MORTA (from *Andrea Chénier*)
Umberto Giordano (1867–1948) . . . . 87
LARGO (from *Clavier Concerto No. 5*)
Johann Sebastian Bach (1685–1750) . . . . 12
MEDITATION (from *Thaïs*)
Jules Massenet (1842–1912) . . . . 82
MINUET AND TRIO (from *String Quintet, Op. 13, No. 5*)
Luigi Boccherini (1743–1805) . . . . 40
MON COEUR S'OUVRE À TA VOIX (from *Samson and Delilah*)
Camille Saint-Saëns (1835–1921) . . . . 52
O MIO BABBINO CARO (from *Gianni Schicchi*)
Giacomo Puccini (1858–1924) . . . . 104
PAVANE
Gabriel Fauré (1845–1924) . . . . 61
POLOVETSIAN DANCE (from *Prince Igor*)
Alexander Borodin (1833–1887) . . . . 106
SOAVE SIA IL VENTO (from *Così Fan Tutte*)
Wolfgang Amadeus Mozart (1756–1791) . . . . 36
THE SWAN (from *Carnival of the Animals*)
Camille Saint-Saëns (1835–1921) . . . . 76
UN BEL DI (from *Madama Butterfly*)
Giacomo Puccini (1858–1924) . . . . 100
VALSE TRISTE
Jean Sibelius (1865–1957) . . . . 92
VOCALISE
Sergei Rachmaninoff (1873–1943) . . . . 112
WALTZ (from *The Sleeping Beauty*)
Peter Ilyich Tchaikovsky (1840–1893) . . . . 116

# Author's Note

The 24 piano transcriptions compiled in this edition were originally published as a series of individual sheet music editions, created over the 18-year period from 1982 to 2000. In December 1995, pianist Tina Faigen recorded 14 of these transcriptions for the ACA Digital compact disc *Tina Faigen Plays Piano Transcriptions.* During the months preceding that recording session, I became convinced of the need to revise my original versions of Albinoni's "Adagio in G Minor" (1991), Bach's "Air" from *Orchestral Suite No. 3* (1993), and Pachelbel's "Canon in D" (1982). Several changes were made to the 1991 version of Albinoni's "Adagio in G Minor," the most important being that the texture supporting each statement of the principal theme became richer and more powerful to enhance the dramatic effect of the entwining melodies. In the 1993 version of Bach's "Air," only the first measure was changed. In the revised version, the transcription begins with the initial melodic tone sustained throughout the entire measure as in Bach's original orchestral version. The transcription of Pachelbel's "Canon in D" was essentially rewritten; remaining intact were only brief segments of the version published in 1982. Faigen recorded the revised versions of these works, and they appeared in print for the first time in the 1998 Warner Bros. Publications' edition *Robert Schultz Piano Transcriptions (EL9801).* Two additional transcriptions were revised for that 1998 edition. The 1982 transcription of Glück's "Dance of the Blessed Spirits" from *Orfeo ed Euridice* appeared in a new engraving with improvements to the editing, and a new transcription of Schubert's "Ave Maria" replaced a version written in 1993.

This updated second edition of *24 Piano Transcriptions of Classical Masterpieces* replaces the prior edition published by Warner Bros. Publications in 2001 (ELM01022). This edition corrects a notation error in "Valse Triste" found in the prior edition. The transcription of Borodin's "Polovetsian Dance" from *Prince Igor,* which did not appear in the first edition, has been included here, as well as the revised versions of the five transcriptions described above.

ROBERT SCHULTZ
February 2008

# ADAGIO IN G MINOR

TOMASO ALBINONI
*Transcribed for Piano by ROBERT SCHULTZ*

mp



© 1998 BELWIN-MILLS PUBLISHING CORP. (ASCAP)
All Rights Administered by WARNER BROS. PUBLICATIONS U.S. INC.
All Rights Reserved including Public Performance for Profit

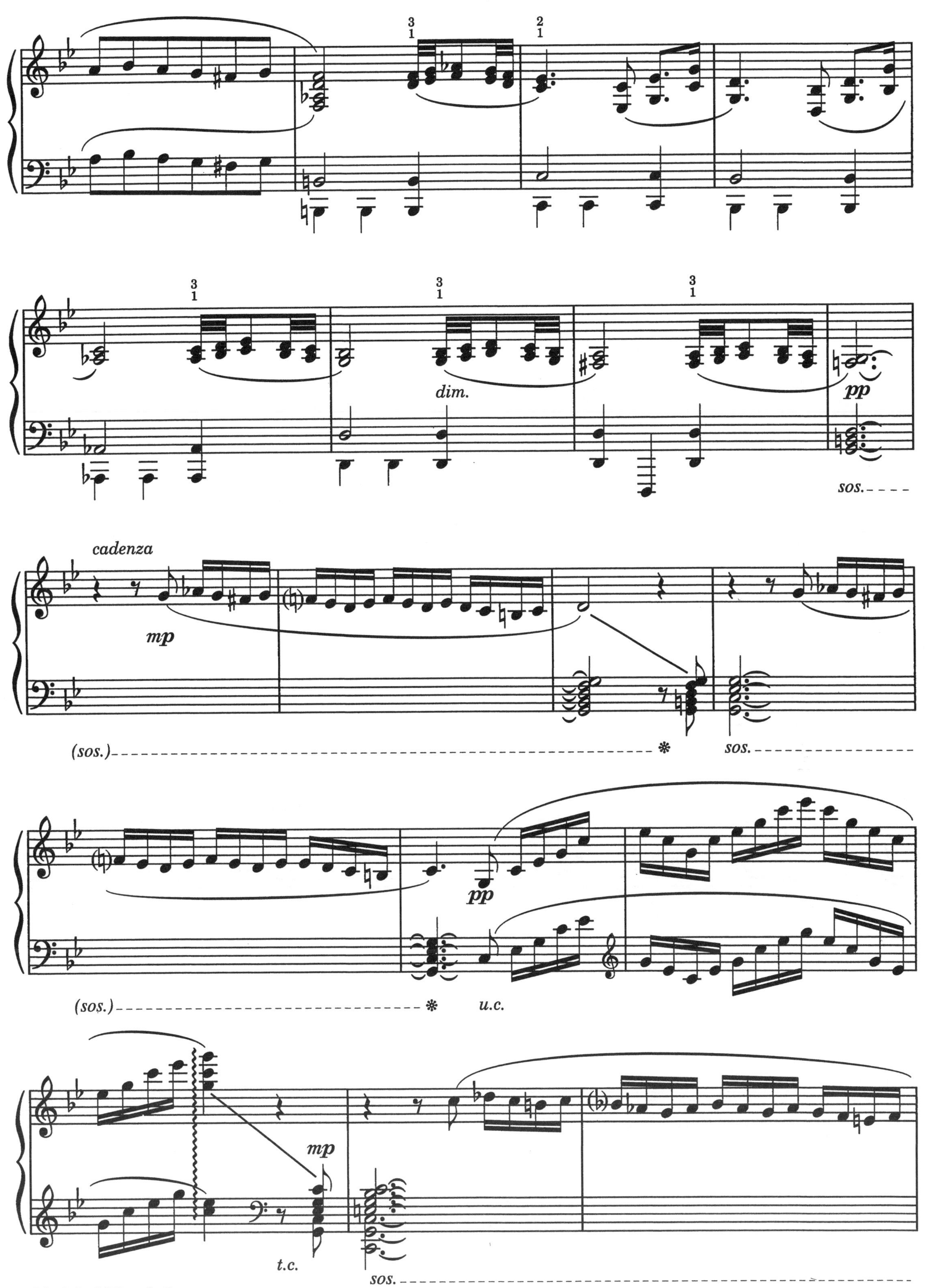

3
1
2
1
3
1
3
1
3
1
dim.
pp
sos.
cadenza
mp
(sos.)
sos.
(sos.)
pp
u.c.
mp
t.c.
sos.

pp
(sos.)
sos.
u.c.

6
6
6
6
3
6
6
6
6
3

mp
t.c.
sos.

f

piú f
mp

3
3
2
1
2-1
5
3-5
3
2
1
mf
f
3
3
1
ff
dim.

mf
f
dim.
p
3
2 3 1
mp
dim. e rit.

# AIR

(from Orchestral Suite No. 3)

JOHANN SEBASTIAN BACH
*Transcribed for Piano by ROBERT SCHULTZ*

© 1998 BELWIN-MILLS PUBLISHING CORP. (ASCAP)
All Rights Administered by WARNER BROS. PUBLICATIONS U.S. INC.
All Rights Reserved including Public Performance for Profit

cresc.
p
tr
cresc.
p
f
mf
dim.
tr

# LARGO

(from Clavier Concerto No. 5)

JOHANN SEBASTIAN BACH
*Transcribed for Piano by ROBERT SCHULTZ*

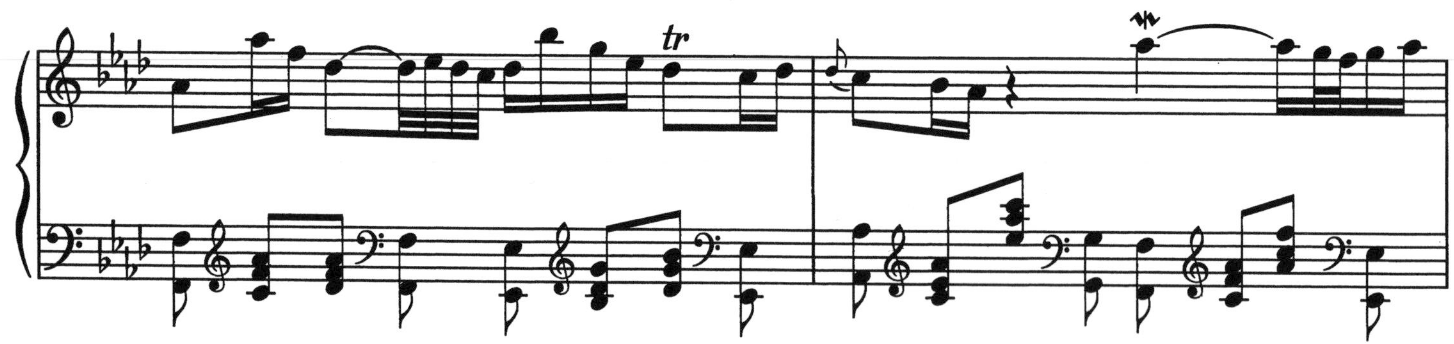

© 1995 BELWIN-MILLS PUBLISHING CORP. (ASCAP)
All Rights Administered by WARNER BROS. PUBLICATIONS U.S. INC.
All Rights Reserved including Public Performance for Profit

tr
3
3
3
3
3

tr

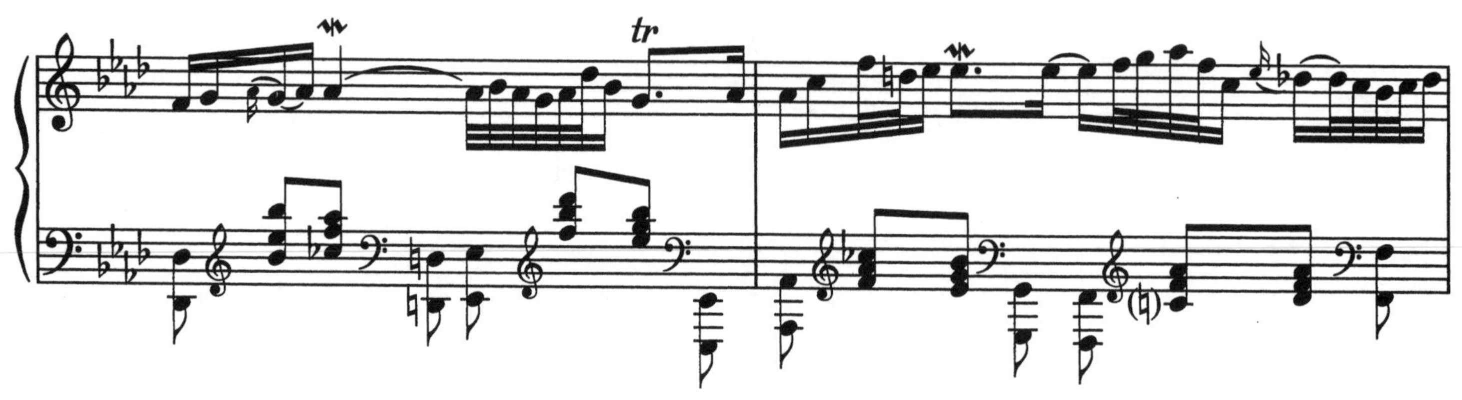
tr
(♮)

tr

# AVE MARIA

GIULIO CACCINI
*Transcribed for Piano by ROBERT SCHULTZ*

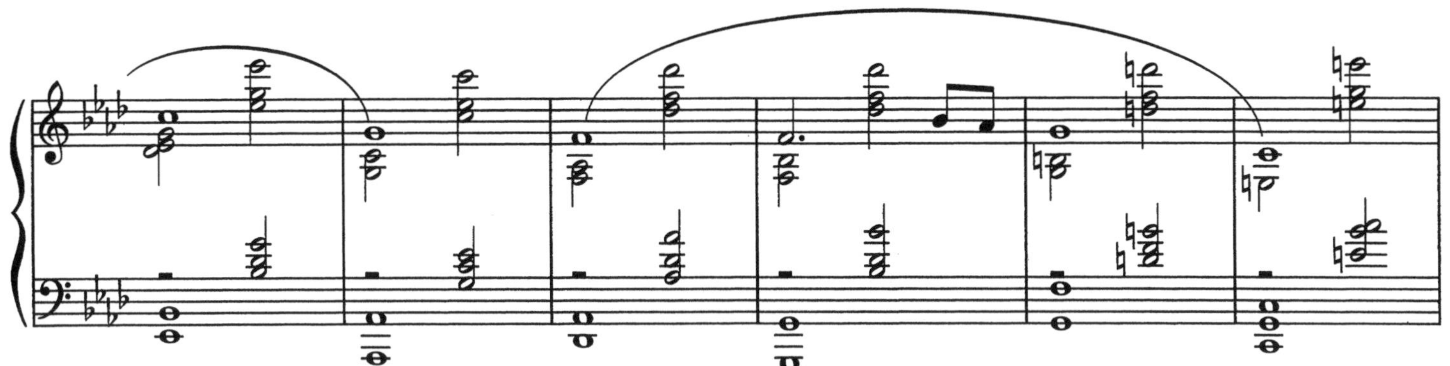



© 1998 BELWIN-MILLS PUBLISHING CORP. (ASCAP)
All Rights Administered by WARNER BROS. PUBLICATIONS U.S. INC.
All Rights Reserved including Public Performance for Profit

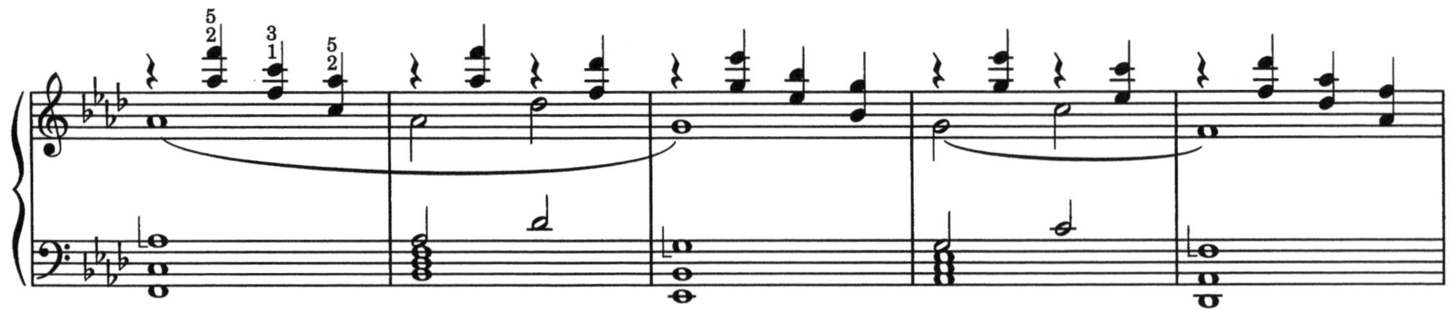
5
2
3
1
5
2

p
mf

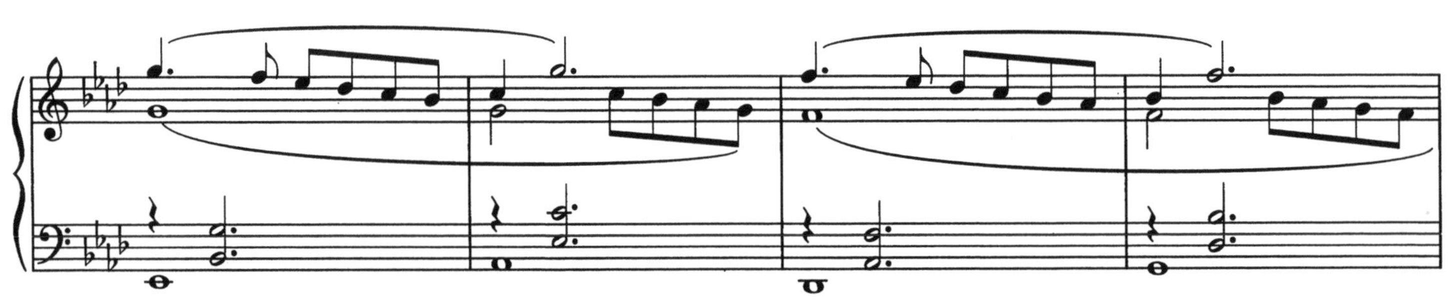

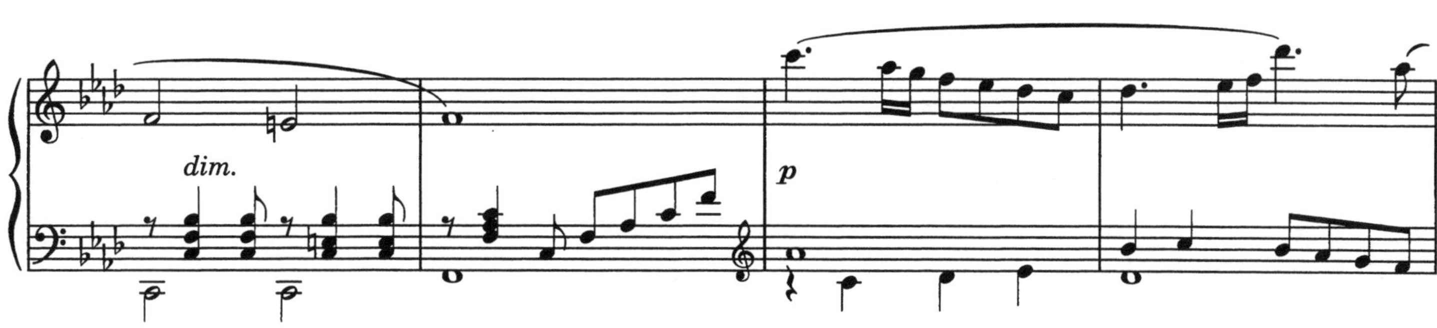
dim.
p

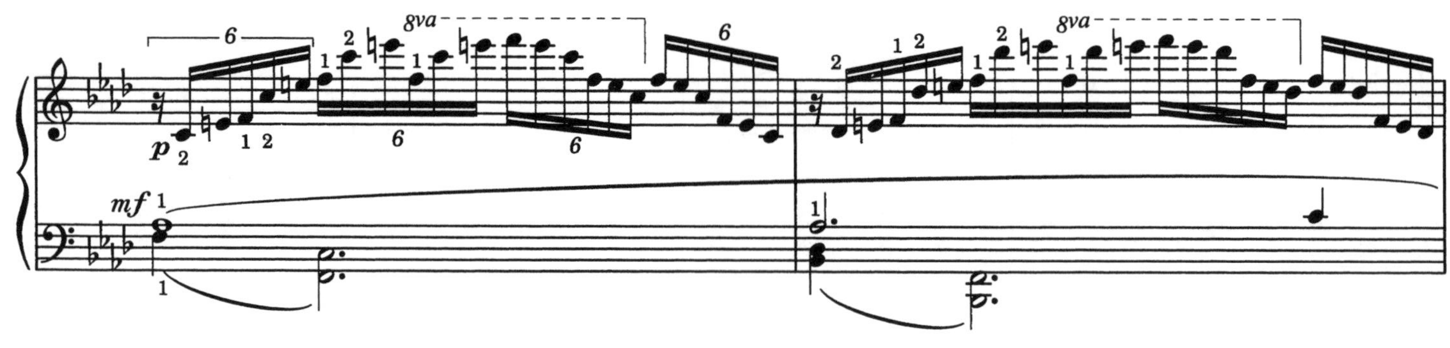
8va
8va
mf
p

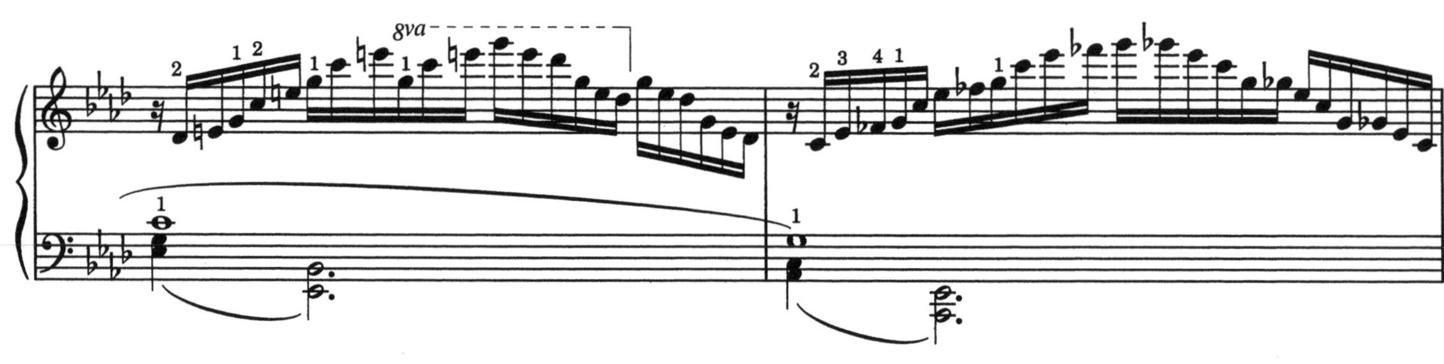
8va

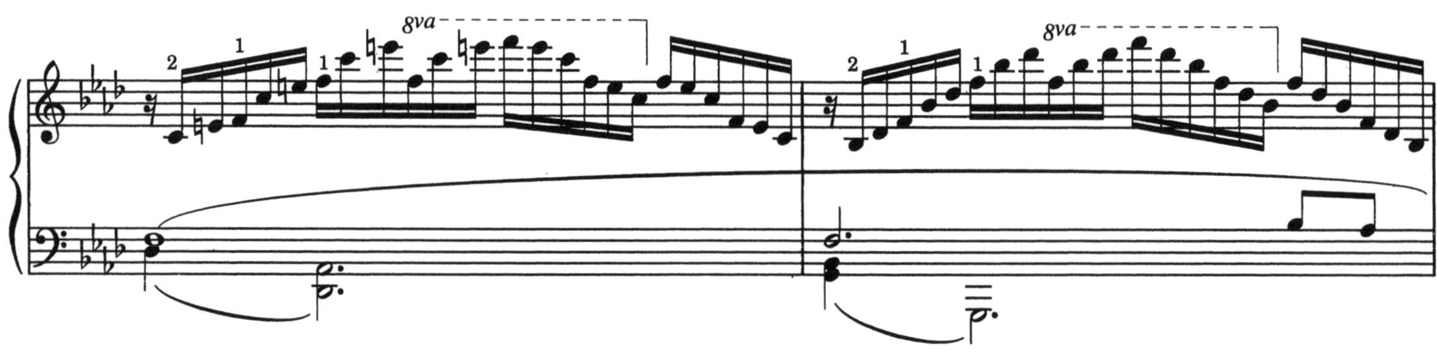
8va
8va

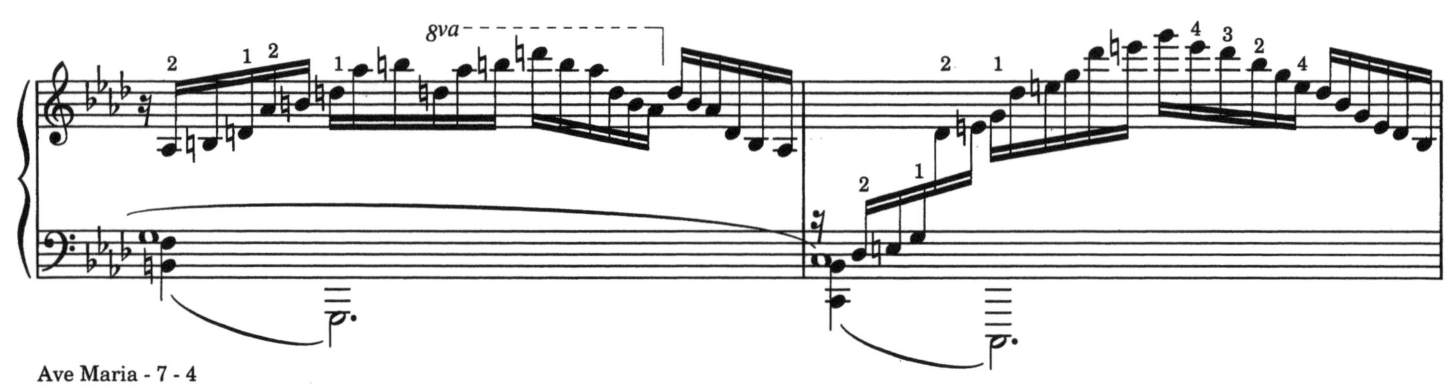
8va

8va
f
8va

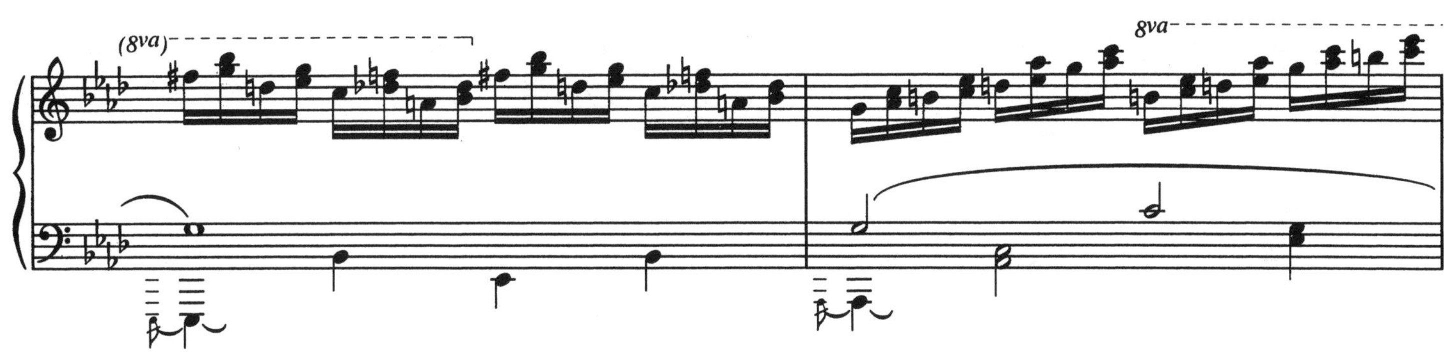
(8va)
8va

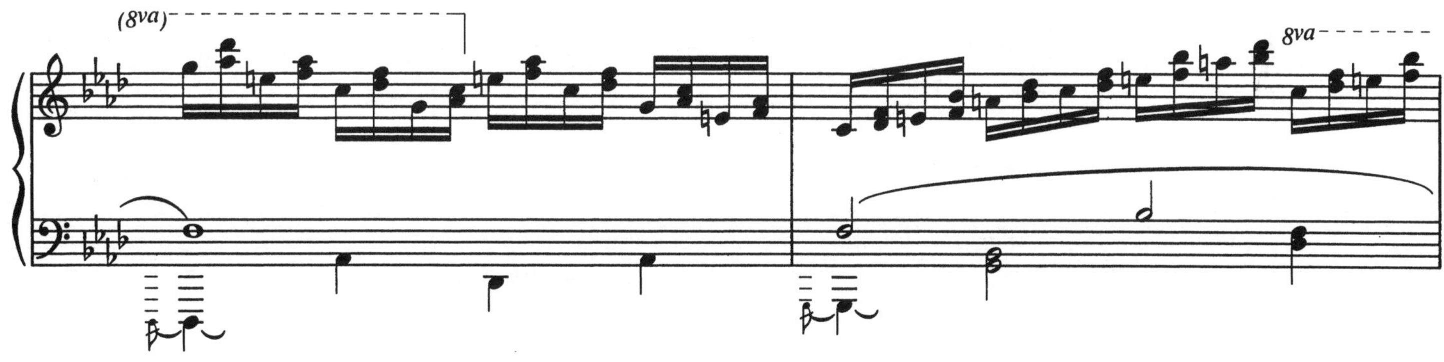
(8va)
8va

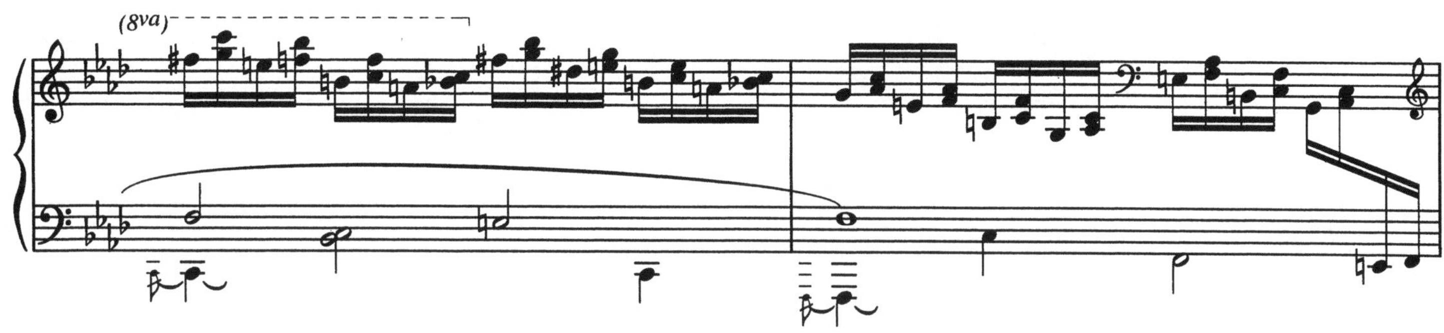
(8va)

più f
5
5
5
5
ff

p
3
2
rit.

# CANON IN D

JOHANN PACHELBEL
*Transcribed for Piano by ROBERT SCHULTZ*

**Moderato grazioso**

© 1998 BELWIN-MILLS PUBLISHING CORP. (ASCAP)
All Rights Administered by WARNER BROS. PUBLICATIONS U.S. INC.
All Rights Reserved including Public Performance for Profit

mp
mf

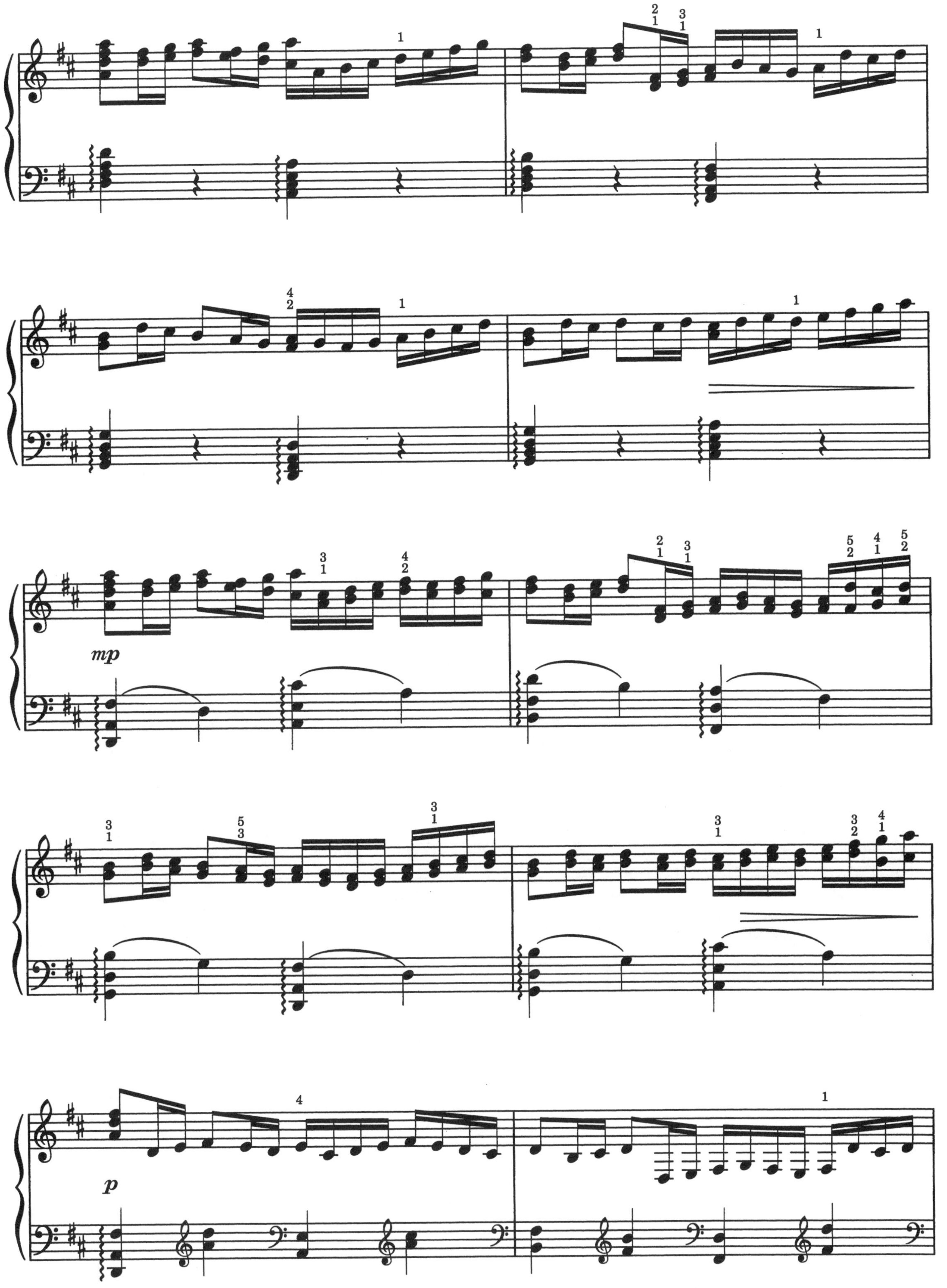
mp
p

4
1

sempre cresc.
f

p
pedal simile
f

dim.
p
(♯)

cresc.
mf

f
rit.

# DANCE OF THE BLESSED SPIRITS
(from Orfeo Ed Euridice)

CHRISTOPH WILLIBALD GLÜCK
*Transcribed for Piano by ROBERT SCHULTZ*

© 1998 BELWIN-MILLS PUBLISHING CORP. (ASCAP)
All Rights Administered by WARNER BROS. PUBLICATIONS U.S. INC.
All Rights Reserved including Public Performance for Profit

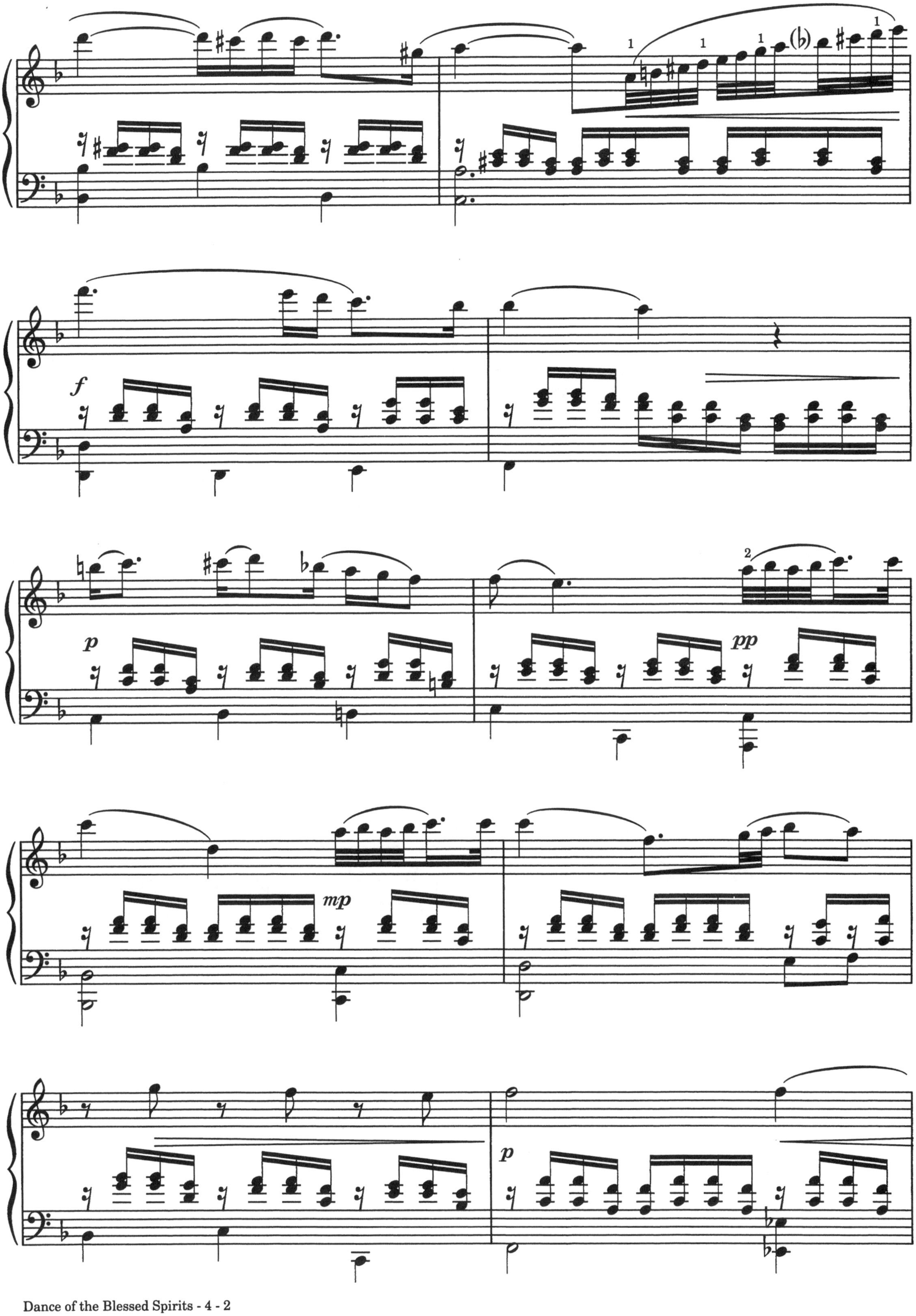

tr
p
pp
mp
cresc.
f
p
f
tr
dim. e rit.

# SOAVE SIA IL VENTO

(from Cosi Fan Tutte)

WOLFGANG AMADEUS MOZART
*Transcribed for Piano by ROBERT SCHULTZ*

© 1994 BELWIN-MILLS PUBLISHING CORP. (ASCAP)
All Rights Administered by WARNER BROS. PUBLICATIONS U.S. INC.
All Rights Reserved including Public Performance for Profit.

2
5
mf

5
3
1

*p*

3

*p*

1
2
5

*cresc.*

5
4
1

*f*

*dim.*

p
p
mp
cresc.
f
p
3
5

# MINUET AND TRIO

(from String Quintet Opus 13, No. 5)

LUIGI BOCCHERINI

*Transcribed for Piano by ROBERT SCHULTZ*

© 1994 BELWIN-MILLS PUBLISHING CORP. (ASCAP)
All Rights Administered by WARNER BROS. PUBLICATIONS U.S. INC.
All Rights Reserved including Public Performance for Profit.

mp
tr
Fine
Trio
p
8va
p

mf
p
8va
D.C. al Fine

# CASTA DIVA
(from Norma)

VINCENZO BELLINI
*Transcribed for Piano by ROBERT SCHULTZ*

© 1997 BELWIN-MILLS PUBLISHING CORP. (ASCAP)
All Rights Administered by WARNER BROS. PUBLICATIONS U.S. INC.
All Rights Reserved including Public Performance for Profit

1
3
mp
cresc.
f
smorz.
sotto voce
p
a tempo

4
2
2
4
2

mp
cresc.

ff
smorz.
a piacére
a tempo
p

# AVE MARIA

FRANZ SCHUBERT
Op. 52, No. 6

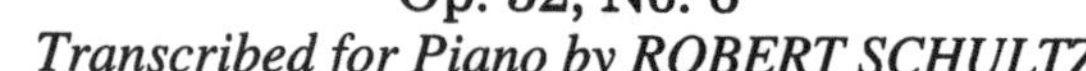

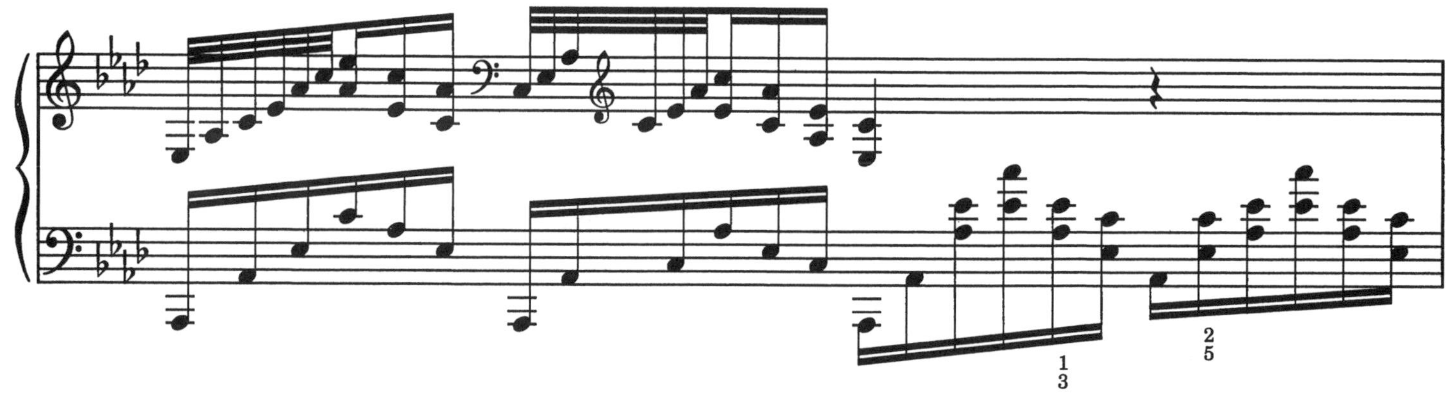

© 1998 BELWIN-MILLS PUBLISHING CORP. (ASCAP)
All Rights Administered by WARNER BROS. PUBLICATIONS U.S. INC.
All Rights Reserved including Public Performance for Profit

6
6
6
2
mp

4
1
3
5
1
3
2
4
6
3
1
mf
3
cresc.
f
dim.
6
p

pp
9

# MON COEUR S'OUVRE A TA VOIX

(My Heart At Thy Sweet Voice)
from *Samson and Delilah*

CAMILLE SAINT-SAËNS
*Transcribed for Piano by* ROBERT SCHULTZ

© 1999 BELWIN-MILLS PUBLISHING CORP. (ASCAP)
All Rights Administered by WARNER BROS. PUBLICATIONS U.S. INC.
All Rights Reserved including Public Performance for Profit

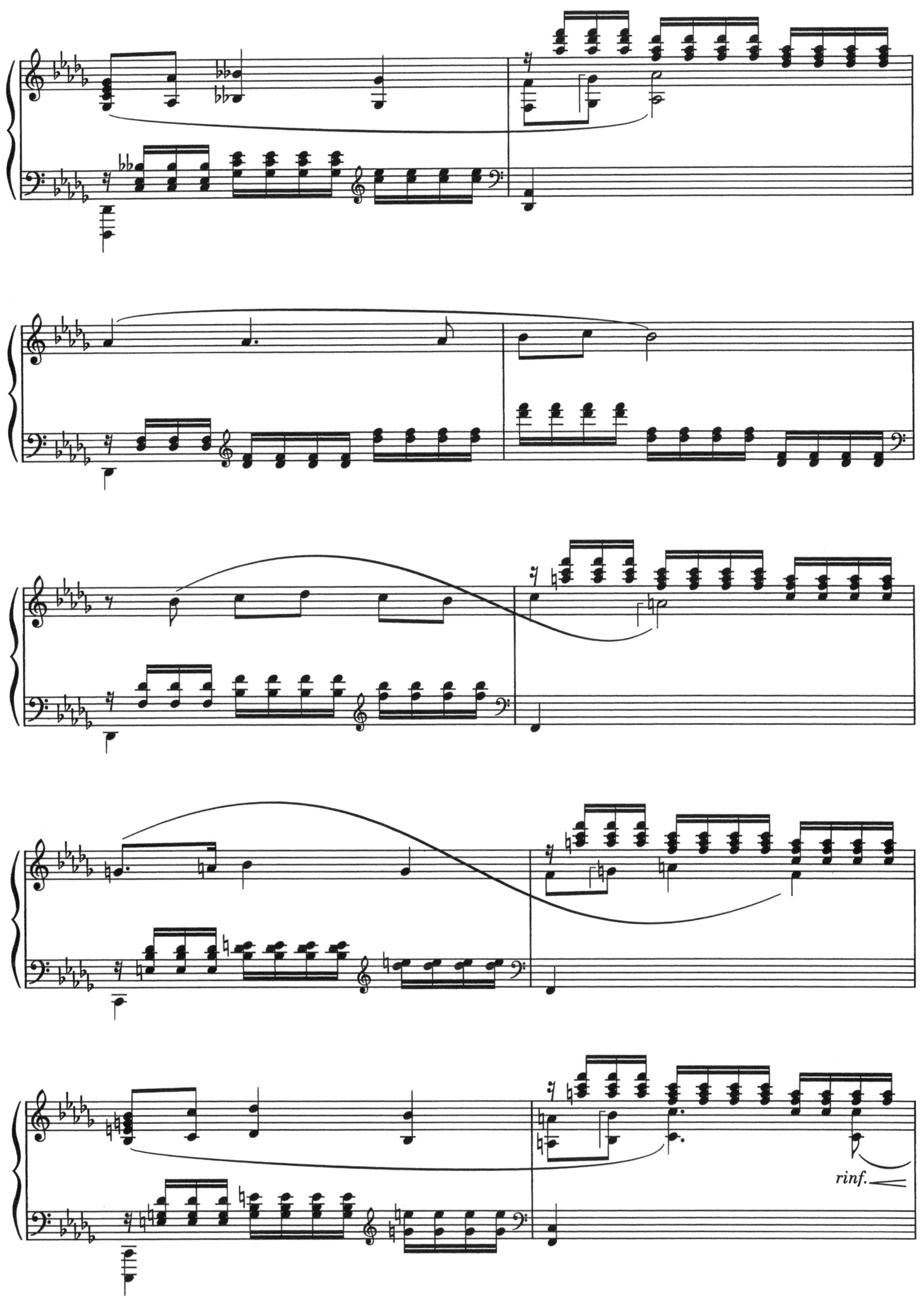
rinf.

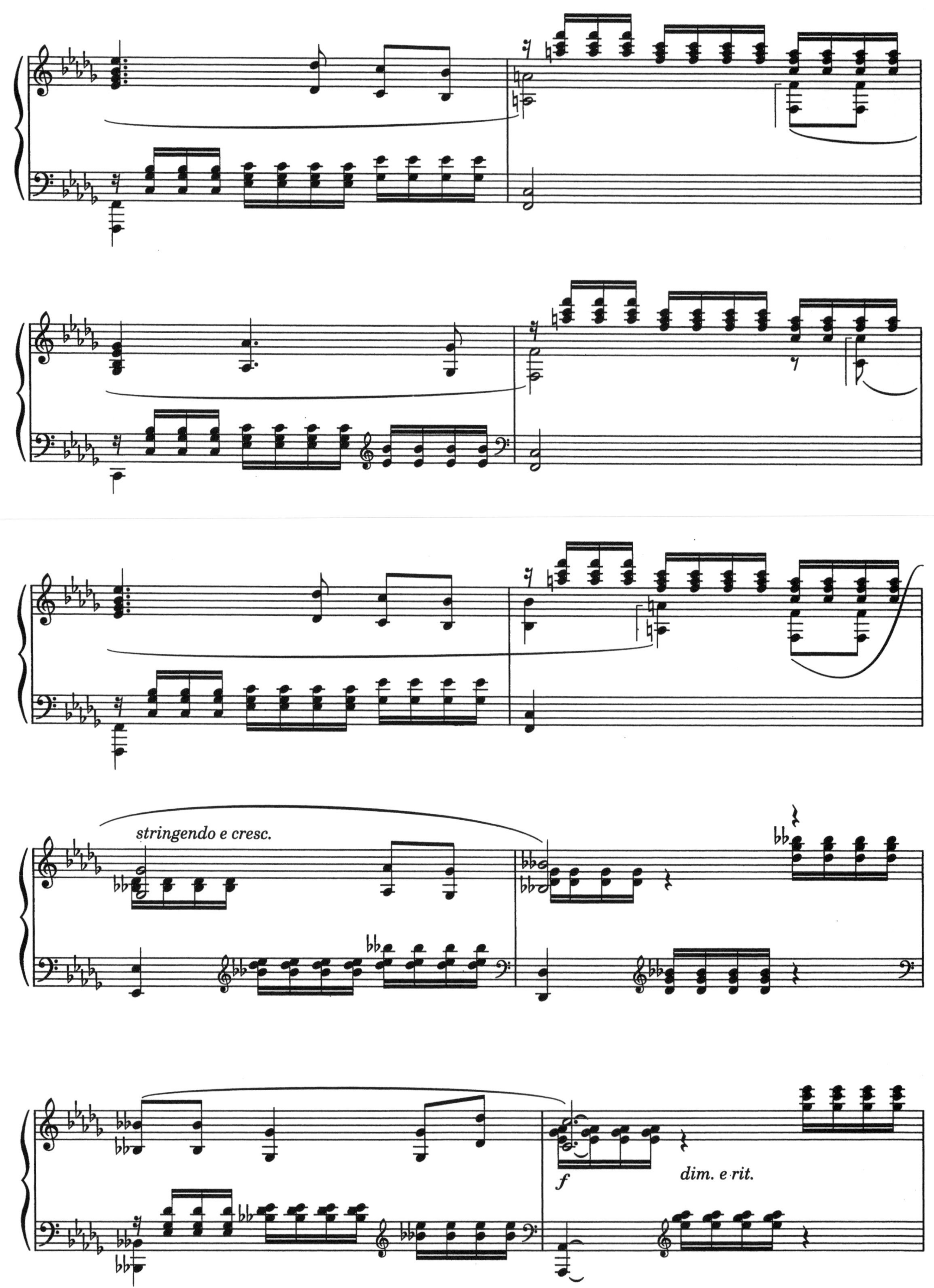
stringendo e cresc.
f
dim. e rit.

Meno mosso
p
(harp)
cresc. senza accel.
f

dim.
p
espr.
espr.
Tempo I
sim.
8va
espressivo

8va
6
6
sim.
1
1

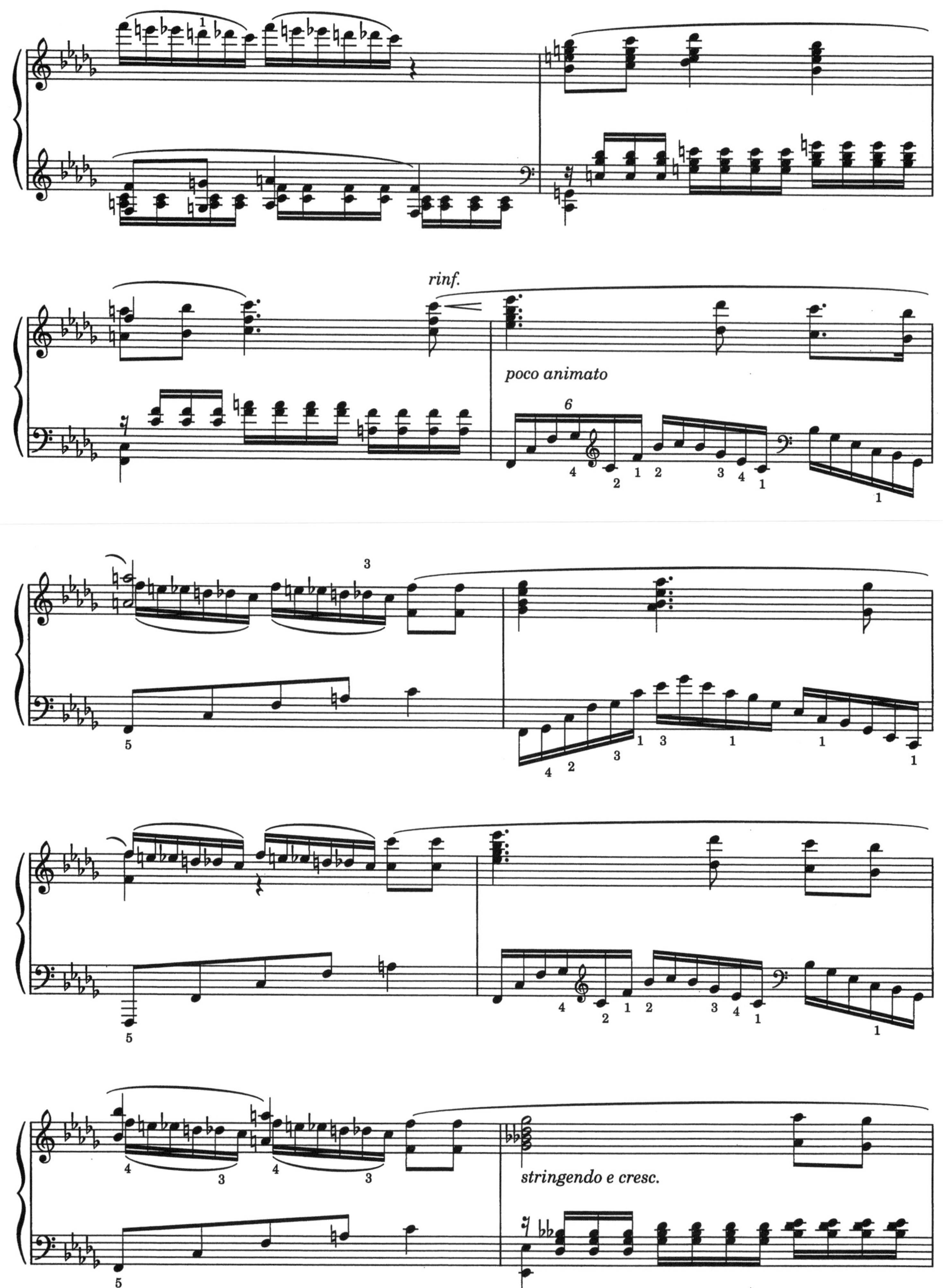
rinf.
poco animato
stringendo e cresc.

f
dim. e rit.
Meno mosso
mp
(harp)
mf

f

ff
8va
dim.

p
espr.
espr.

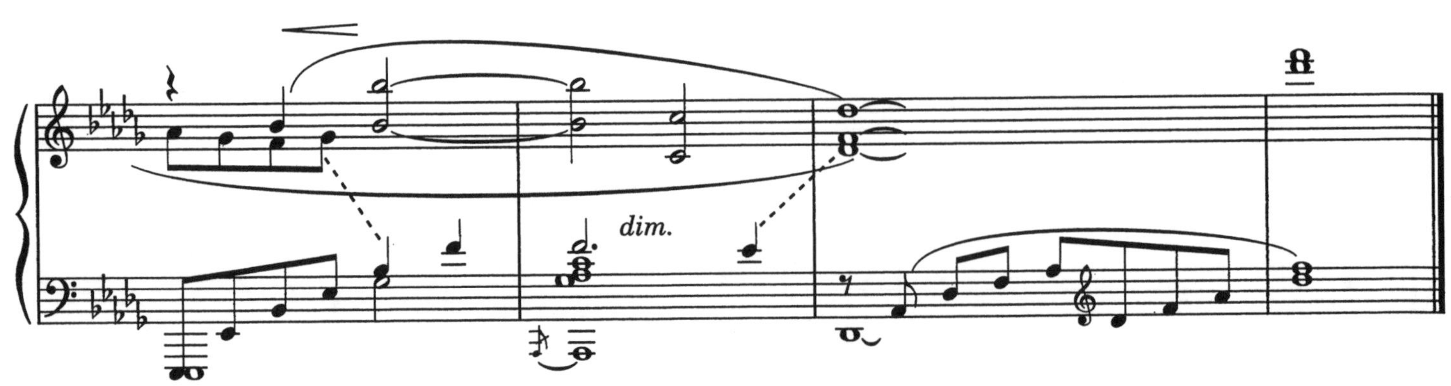
dim.

# PAVANE

GABRIEL FAURÉ, Op. 50
*Transcribed for Piano by ROBERT SCHULTZ*

© 1989 BEAM ME UP MUSIC (ASCAP)
All Rights Administered by WARNER BROS. PUBLICATIONS U.S. INC.
All Rights Reserved including Public Performance for Profit.

Ped.
Ped.
tr
mp

Ped. Ped. *

f
mp
sos.
*

dolce
tr

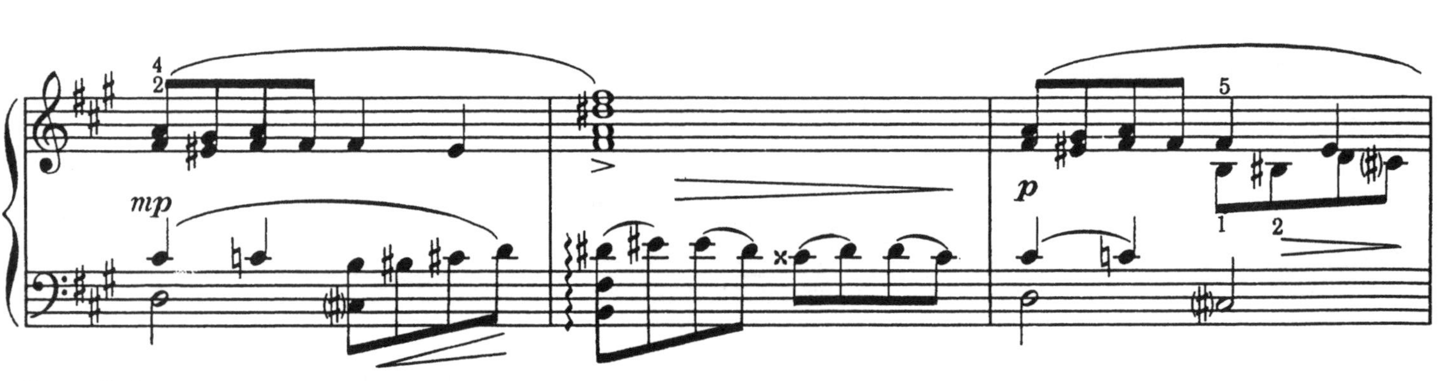
mf
Ped.
Ped.
Ped.
Ped.
Ped.
Ped.
Ped.
Ped.
Ped.
Ped.
mp
p
*
mf
mp
p

pp
mp espressivo
Ped.
mf
p
mp
l.h.
u.c.
ppp

# KOL NIDREI

MAX BRUCH, Op. 47
*Transcribed for Piano by ROBERT SCHULTZ*

**Adagio non troppo**

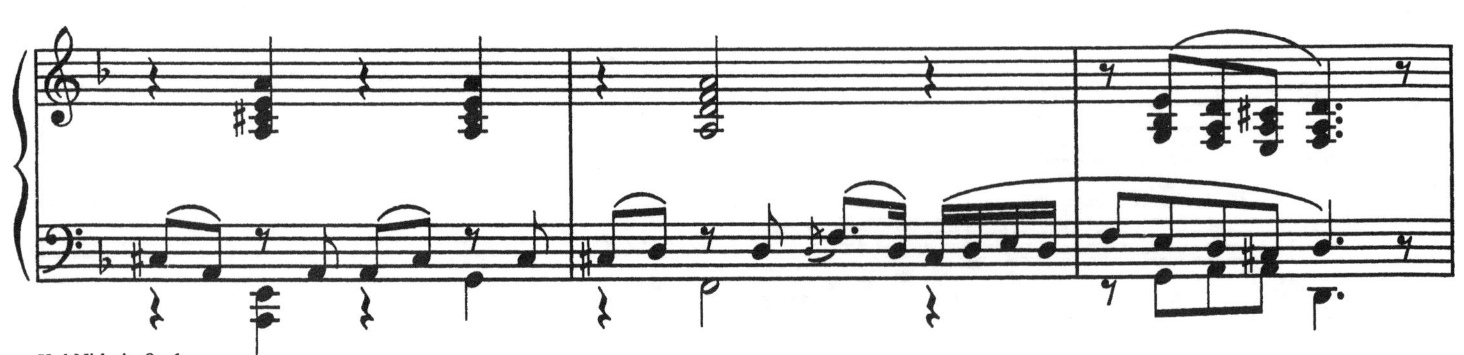



© 1994 BELWIN-MILLS PUBLISHIG CORP. (ASCAP)
All Rights Administered by WARNER BROS. PUBLICATIONS U.S. INC.
All Rights Reserved including Public Performance for Profit.

mp
p
mp
mf
5
dim.
p
f
3
3
mp

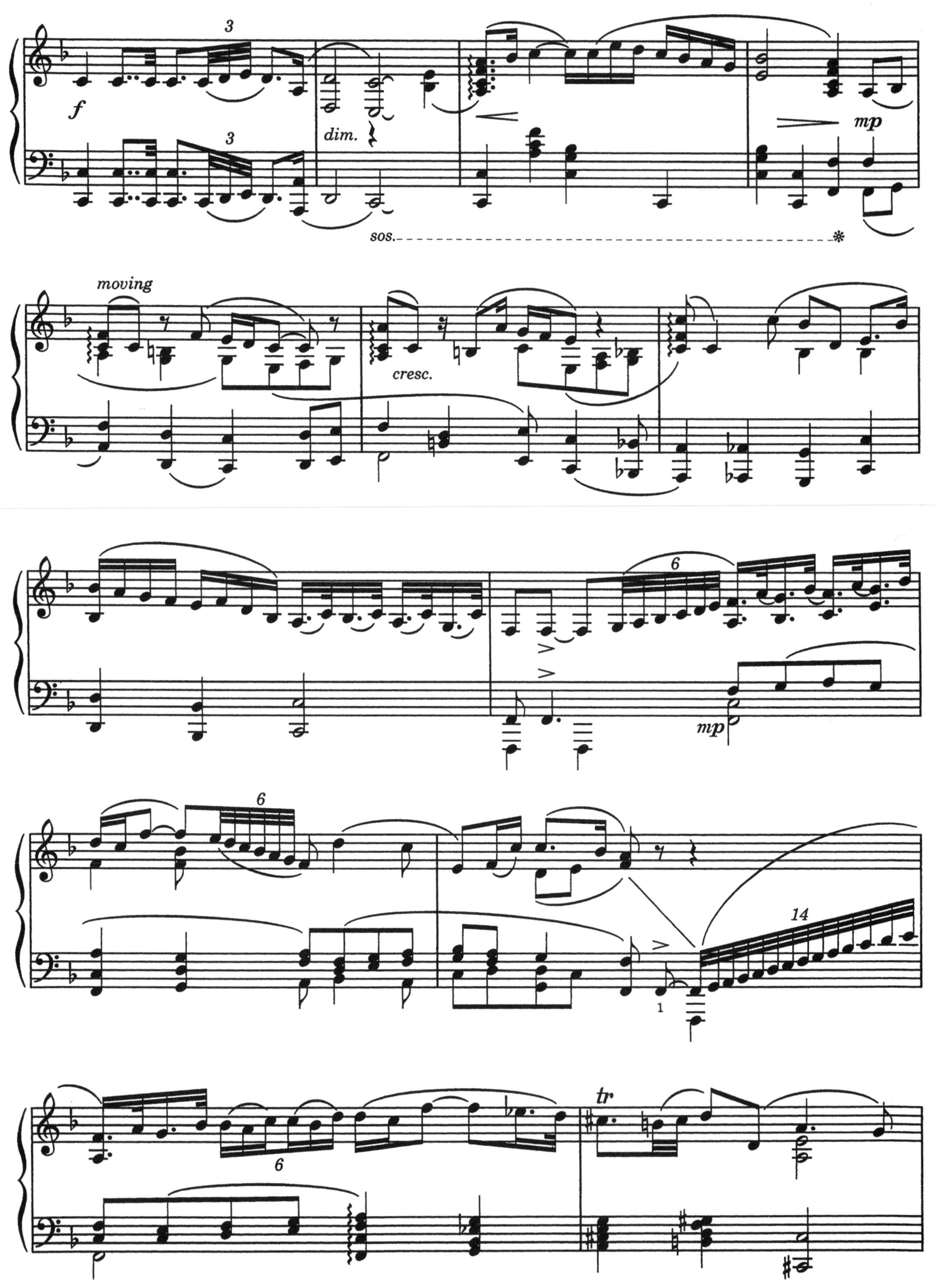
3
3
f
dim.
sos.
mp
moving
cresc.
6
mp
6
14
1
6
tr

tr
mf
p
pp
mp

mf
3
p
6
pizz.
p
mf
mf

1
mf
3
5
mf
f
mf

p
dim.
mf
p
tr
mp

pp
pizz.
p
pp
pizz.
pp
pp
pizz.
l.h.
morendo
p
pp

# THE SWAN
(from Carnival of the Animals)

CAMILLE SAINT-SAËNS
*Transcribed for Piano by ROBERT SCHULTZ*

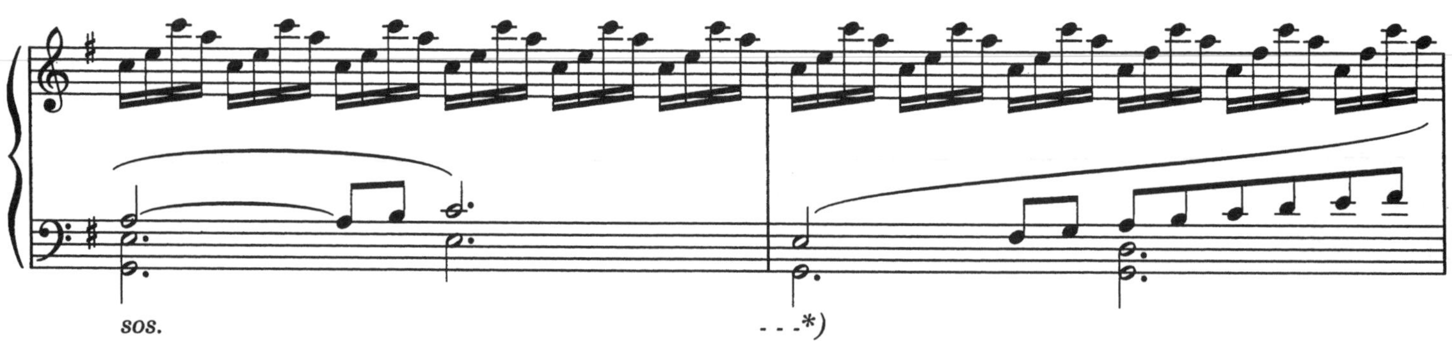


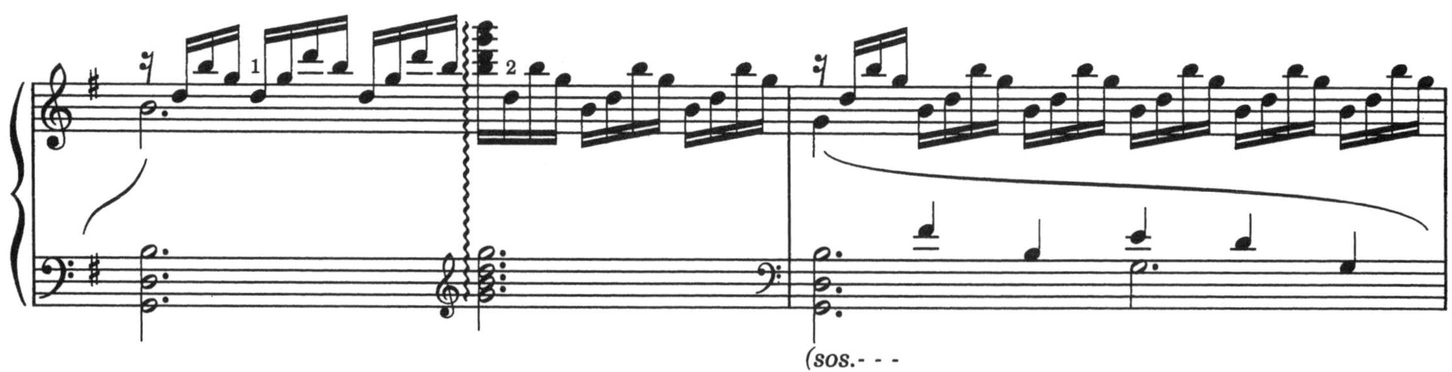


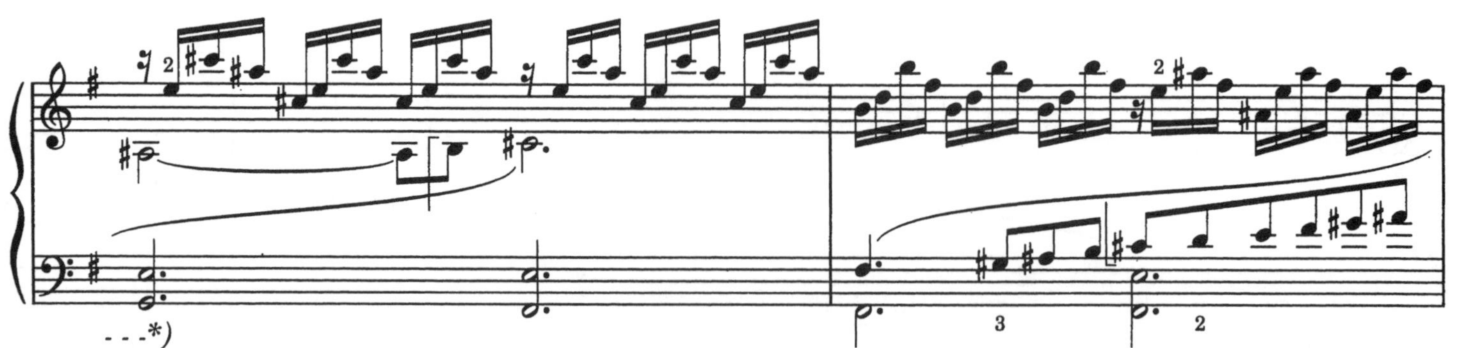




© 1995 BELWIN-MILLS PUBLISHING CORP. (ASCAP)
All Rights Administered by WARNER BROS. PUBLICATIONS U.S. INC.
All Rights Reserved including Public Performance for Profit.

8va
8va
8va
8va
p
(sos.- - -

sos.
- - -*)
f
1
pp
8va
sos.- - -
rit.

# INTERMEZZO

(from Cavalleria Rusticana)

PIETRO MASCAGNI

*Transcribed for Piano by ROBERT SCHULTZ*

**Andante sostenuto ♩ = 56**



© 1994 BELWIN-MILLS PUBLISHING CORP.(ASCAP)
All Rights Administered by WARNER BROS. PUBLICATIONS U.S. INC.
All Rights Reserved including Public Performance for Profit

Poco più mosso ♩ = 80-92
p
rall.
pizz.
f

mp
f
mp
f
rall. e dim. sempre
dim.
p
morendo
Ped.
*

# MEDITATION
(from the opera *Thaïs*)

JULES MASSENET
*Transcribed for Piano by ROBERT SCHULTZ*

**Andante religioso**

© 1994 BELWIN-MILLS PUBLISHING CORP. (ASCAP)
All Rights Administered by WARNER BROS. PUBLICATIONS U.S. INC.
All Rights Reserved including Public Performance for Profit

mf
mp
dim. e rit.
Poco più mosso
p
a tempo
mf
cresc.
f
mp
cresc.

Più mosso agitato
Tempo I
f
più f
ff
8va
rit.
mp
dim. e poco rit.
3
5

rall.
a tempo
3
cresc.
8va
f
3
dim. e rit.

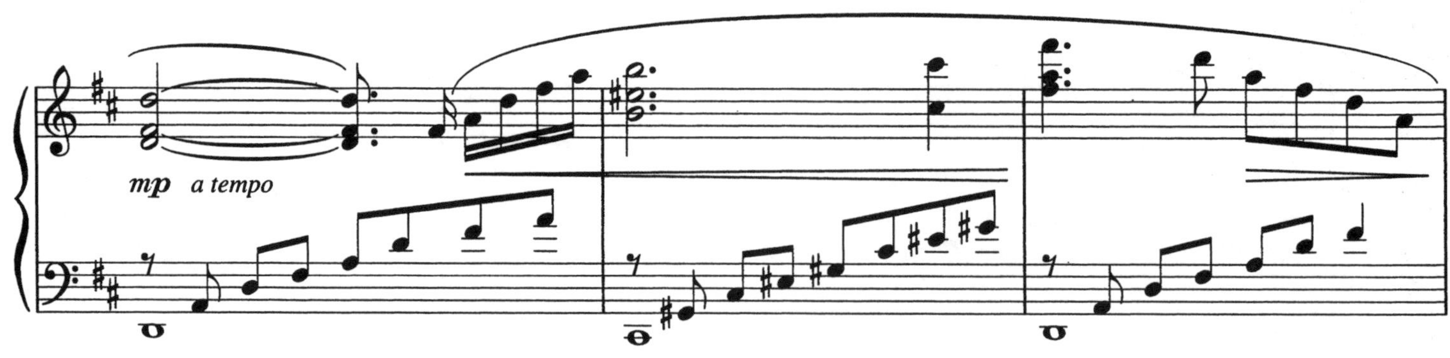
mp a tempo

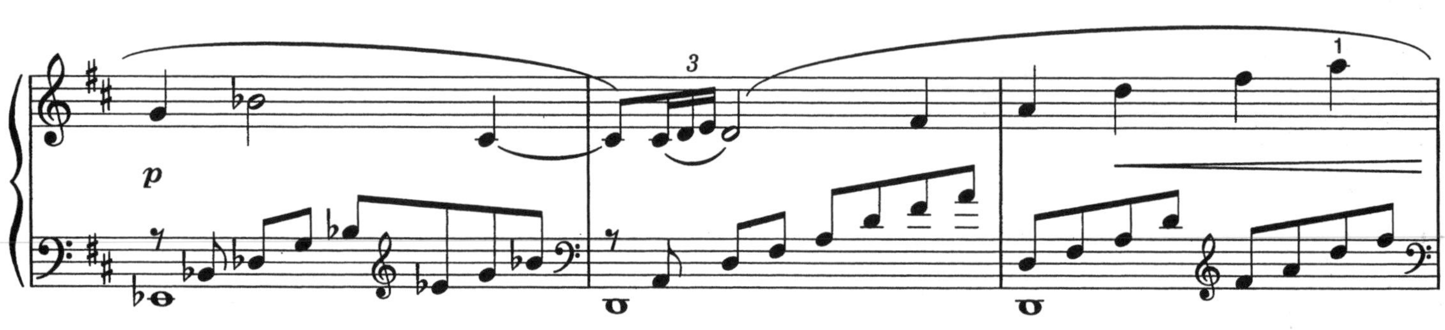
3
1
p

mp
dim.

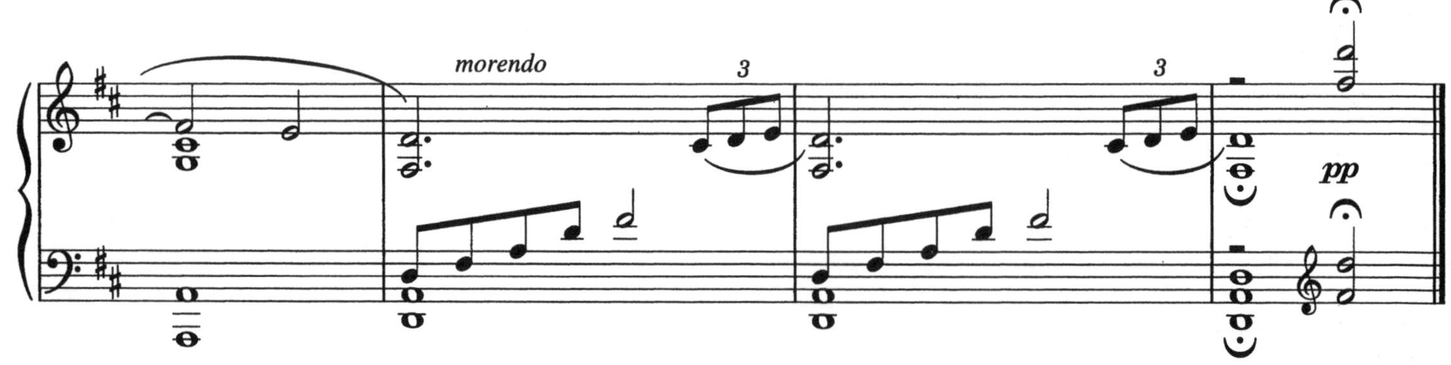
morendo
3
3
pp

# LA MAMMA MORTA
(from Andrea Chénier)

UMBERTO GIORDANO
*Transcribed for Piano by ROBERT SCHULTZ*

**Slowly, solemnly**

© 1994 BELWIN-MILLS PUBLISHING CORP. (ASCAP)
All Rights Administerd by WARNER BROS. PUBLICATIONS U.S. INC.
All Rigths Reserved including Public Performance for Profit.

accel.
Più mosso (♩ = 108)
8va
f
Meno mosso
p
dim.
mp
pp
ppp
mf moving

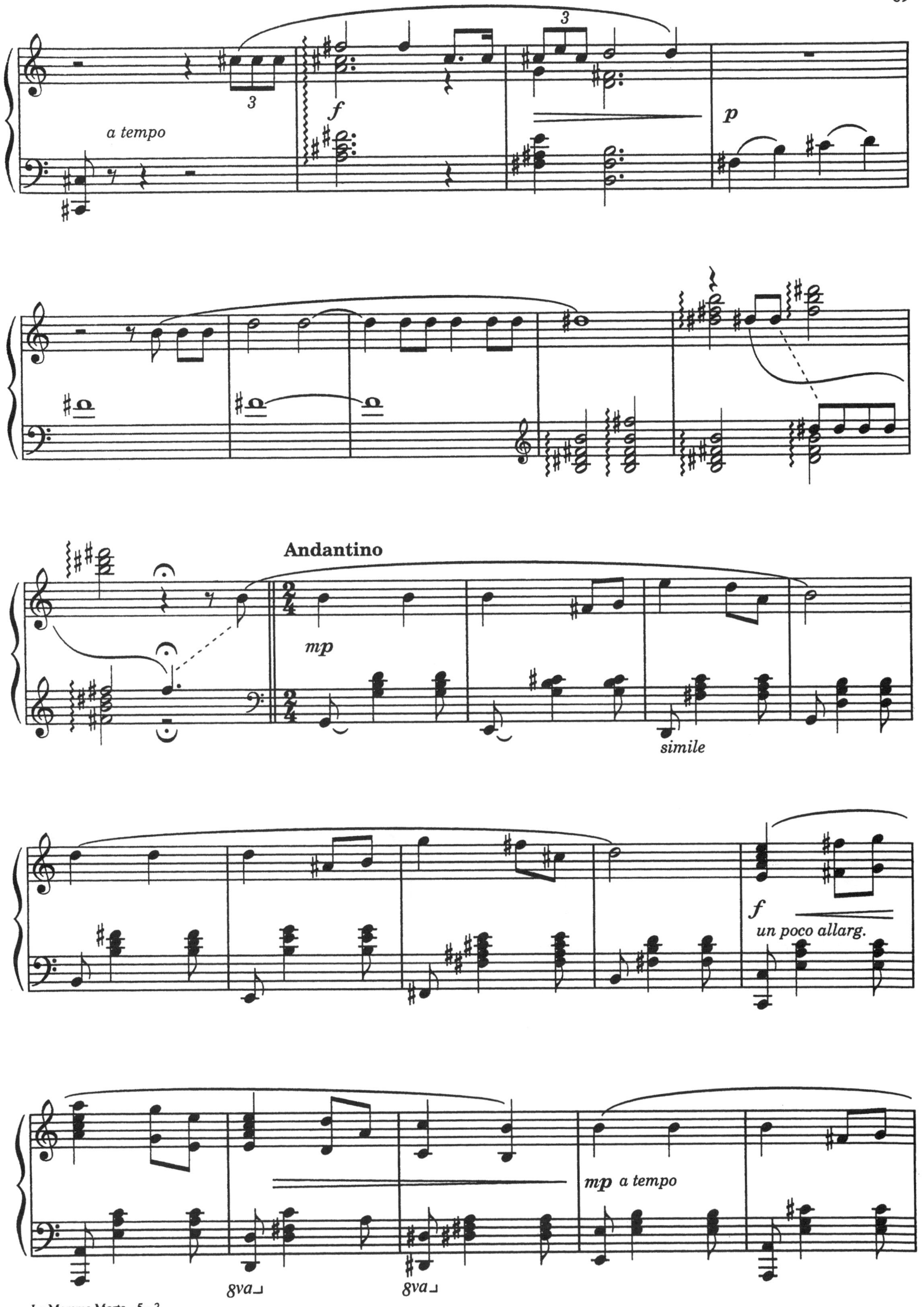
a tempo
f
p
Andantino
mp
simile
f
un poco allarg.
8va
8va
mp a tempo

poco più animato
3
8va
ff
Ped.
Più mosso
p
mp
*

1
2
3
4
cresc.
f
3
4
4
Più mosso (♩ = 112)
f
pedal simile
cresc.
ff
poco rit.
8va
f
rit.
3
8va

# VALSE TRISTE

JEAN SIBELIUS
Op. 44
*Transcribed for Piano by ROBERT SCHULTZ*

© 1996 BELWIN-MILLS PUBLISHING CORP. (ASCAP)
All Rights Administered by WARNER BROS. PUBLICATIONS U.S. INC.
All Rights Reserved including Public Performance for Profit

8va
(8va)
rall.
p
a tempo
(8va)

poco rall.
a tempo
dim.
espressivo
mp

p
cresc.
f
dim. molto
pp
mp
8va
Lento
rit.
pp
(8va)

p a tempo
mp
p cresc.
f

Poco risoluto
f
cresc.
ff
3

3
Piú risoluto e mosso
Stretto
8va
(8va)
(8va)

(8va)
(8va)
(8va)
Lento assai
meno f
dim.
(8va)
8va
pp
pp
Ped.
Ped.
Ped.
Ped.

# UN BEL DI

(from Madama Butterfly)

GIACOMO PUCCINI
*Transcribed for Piano by ROBERT SCHULTZ*

© 1998 BELWIN-MILLS PUBLISHING CORP. (ASCAP)
All Rights Administered by WARNER BROS. PUBLICATIONS U.S. INC.
All Rights Reserved including Public Performance for Profit

un poco mosso
mf
ritenuto
f
mp
rall.
p
a tempo
rit.
a tempo
mp
ritenuto

a tempo
p
sos.
sos.
poco rall.
meno mosso
pp
rall.
Tempo I
f
rit.
a tempo

poco agitato
mp
p
f
cresc. e poco rall.
12
a tempo
fff
dim.
rall.

# O MIO BABBINO CARO

(from Gianni Schicchi)

GIACOMO PUCCINI
*Transcribed for Piano by ROBERT SCHULTZ*

© 1998 BELWIN-MILLS PUBLISHING CORP. (ASCAP)
All Rights Administered by WARNER BROS. PUBLICATIONS U.S. INC.
All Rights Reserved including Public Performance for Profit

*mp*

*mf*

*ritenuto*

*a tempo*

*f*

*rit.*

**Slower**

*p*

# POLOVETSIAN DANCE

(from Prince Igor)

ALEXANDER BORODIN
*Transcribed for Piano by ROBERT SCHULTZ*

© 1996 BELWIN-MILLS PUBLISHING CORP. (ASCAP)
All Rights Administered by WARNER BROS. PUBLICATIONS U.S. INC.
All Rights Reserved including Public Performance for Profit

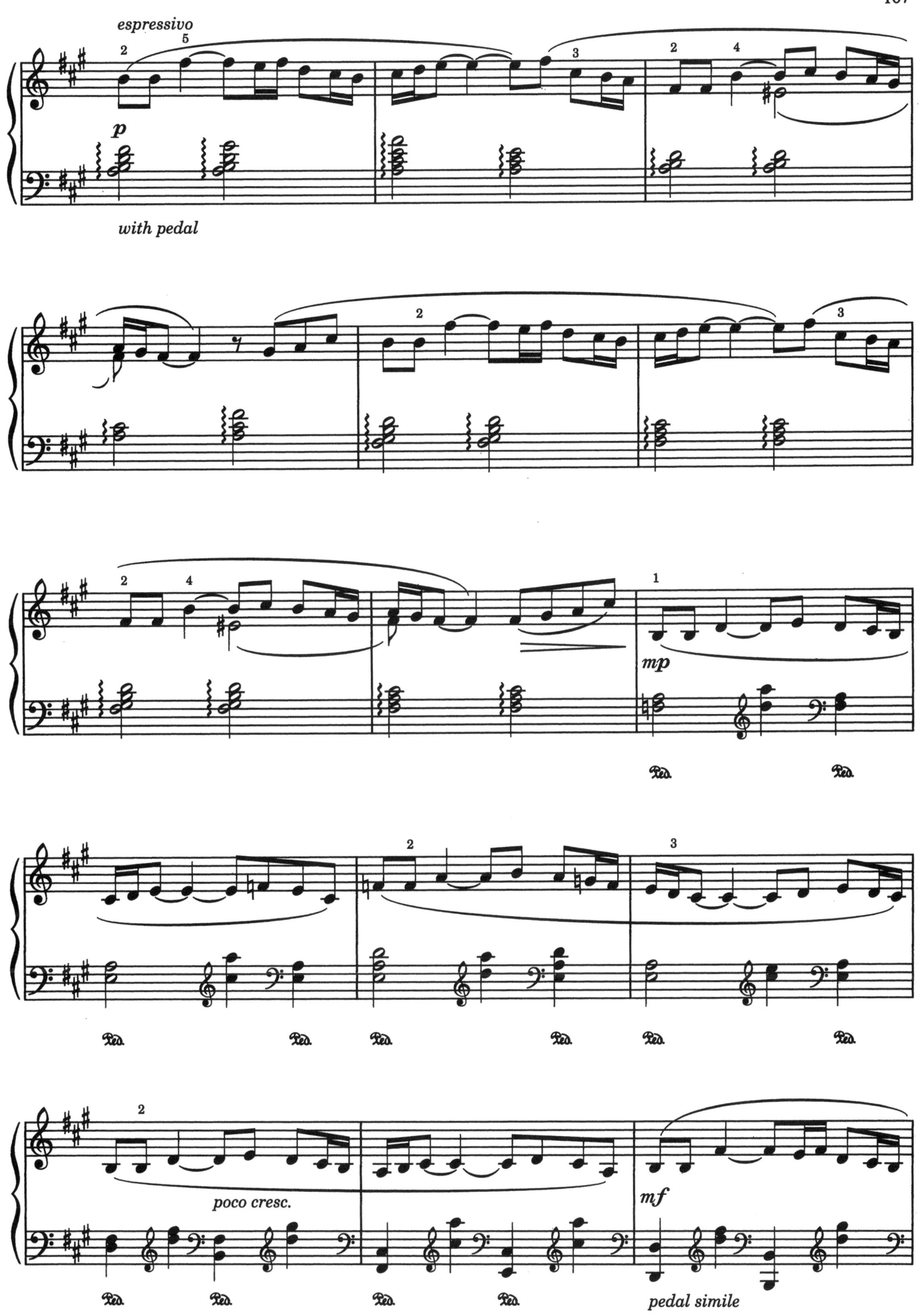
espressivo
p
with pedal
mp
poco cresc.
mf
pedal simile

f
dim. poco a poco
pp

# EIGHTEENTH VARIATION

(from Rhapsody on a Theme of Paganini)

SERGEI RACHMANINOFF

*Transcribed for Piano by ROBERT SCHULTZ*

© 1953 by Charles Foley, Inc.
Copyright Renewed
All Rights Assigned to and Administered by BOOSEY & HAWKES MUSIC PUBLISHERS LTD (Publishing)
and WARNER BROS. PUBLICATIONS U.S. INC. (Print)
All Rights Reserved including Public Performance for Profit

1
1
f
2
3
5
5
ff

dim. poco a poco
p
dim. e rit.

# VOCALISE

SERGEI RACHMANINOFF, Op. 34, No. 14
*Transcribed for Piano by ROBERT SCHULTZ*

© 1991 BEAM ME UP MUSIC (ASCAP)
All Rights Administered by WARNER BROS. PUBLICATIONS U.S. INC.
All Rights Reserved including Public Performance for Profit.

p
mf
mp
pp
1.
2.
poco più mosso
mp

mf
mp

poco rit.
1.
poco più mosso
pp
mp
2.
p
mp
pp
(p)
cresc.
dim.
tr
p
mp
pp
p
pp

# WALTZ

(from The Sleeping Beauty)

PETER ILYICH TCHAIKOVSKY
*Transcribed for Piano by ROBERT SCHULTZ*

© 1999 BELWIN-MILLS PUBLISHING CORP. (ASCAP)
All Rights Administered by WARNER BROS. PUBLICATIONS U.S. INC.
All Rights Reserved including Public Performance for Profit

p
p

cresc.
f
ff
mf

2
2
ff
mf
ff
mf
ff
mf

dim.
p
8va
Waltz - 9 - 5

8va
f
piú f
dim.
p
espressivo

8va
(8va)
(8va)
cresc.
(8va)
f
8va
mp
8va
(8va)
8va
8va

(8va)
8va
8va
(8va)
8va
8va
(8va)
8va
8va
(8va)
8va
5 3 2 3 2
8va
(8va)
f
1
ff

8va
1
2
3
1
8va
1
1
1
1
8va
8va
8va
8va
8va